FRENCH DAYS, FRENCH VOICES

Wendy Lee

Another sky

Special Advisor Douglas Callaway.

For Julian and Jonathan Lee, with love.

Explanation.

Most people have long had a love affair with France. Everyone wants a holiday there.

It is a spectacular country: beautiful villages, luminous cities, dark blue seas and skies, snow-covered mountains, limitless space…

They say you can be skiing in the mountains in the morning and sunbathing on a beach in the afternoon.

It's no wonder the French hardly ever leave it.

But.. this is a story about the experience of something more rare. This is living in, what to me as an English woman will always be someone else's country, to be 'une étrangère', but not a holiday maker, nor part of an 'Expat' community.

I don't mention, or not intentionally, perfect beaches, restaurants, sunbathing, or numbers of days of sun.

Living now in the heart of a French village, surrounded by French neighbours, this is a different place: a morning chat in the street, perhaps about the wind or heat, a glance at the local French paper, a conversation late on a hot afternoon sitting under the lime tree. A slightly different world view.

To say this is a true picture of France is naive, but in talking to my neighbours, I have tried to use understanding in my story.

I write observations of daily life - without too much 'me'. The use of 'the man, woman or dog' is cumbersome, but more impartial than 'we' or 'I'. The illustrations and poetry are to explain, when I cannot!

I hope not to be too critical or too rose coloured, but simply objective. A reporter not an opinion writer.

How successful I have been I leave for the reader to judge.

Wendy Lee, France 2024

P. S. In these post-Brexit days I am hoping that British people will still have opportunities to live (and work) in France.

As I write this, in 2024, British Airways are reinstating some flights to Nice, so….

Table of Contents.

The backstory. 1

'Another Sky' or 'Oh, Monoculture!' 5

'Arrival,' or 'A Room with a View.'. 12

'A Farewell' or 'Not sure about the Health and Safety.' 19

'Desiderata' Max Ehrmann, or 'Back to Base.'. 27

'Sea Fever John Masefield, or 'This boat has a value y'know.' 30

'Afternoon on a hill, or 'The Enchantment.' 37

'I taught myself to live simply' or 'What do you do all day, sunbathe?' 49

'Acquainted with the night' Robert Frost   or 'L'heure Bleue.' 111

'Life and 'The Coming of Good Luck.' Robert Herrick 141

The backstory.

They say never begin a story with the weather('it was a dark and stormy night'....) but, no matter, this tale begins in cold midwinter at the Millennium.

Most things begin with a story - most things usually do.

A man and woman, friends from long ago, now find themselves on the same wavelength, or so they think.

Proud of their careers in science and health, marriages and grown -up families, life has been good. But they are a new couple, neither young- nor old enough to know better. This is foolhardy and impulsive. The woman knows that she can 'leap before she looks'.

This could be called an adventure, or maybe just escapism.

The woman hopes the man hasn't become too serious, scientists tend to be serious people, you don't see them dancing on tables much.

If you ask what they expect, the answer would probably be who knows?, but they like the idea of life in a different country, a new environment, village life-perhaps café culture

'I want to practise sitting outside a café, watching the world go by', says the man.

They hope French people will talk to them.

'To really know a place you have to know the people, one at a time -and come to your own conclusions, ' says the woman, (or so she has read).

They know their school French is not conversational. It is more about grammar and conjugating verbs - and a long time ago. They are not Francophiles, and have no pretensions to say they dream in French. Never mind. A little bit of Frenchness could do them good.

'Celebrity people gravitate towards America, thinking people live in France', says the man - for no particular reason.

The are warned by those with more wisdom that they will always feel like nomads, not quite at home in two countries, just forever between the two, forever time-travellers. Maybe… for company, they take the dog.

Bon Voyage

It's surprising that this new environment is only a shortish hop from England, and bordered to the north by the English Channel. 'Ninety nine nautical miles from the West Country', says the man, and from now on to be called 'La Manche.'

The ferry is big enough to call itself a cruise ship, but not an ocean liner, which seems appropriate.

The decks are many, the cabins hard to find, the passageways never ending, but the couple are optimistic. The sea looks 'flat calm' says the man, (a nautical type, and no stranger to blue or grey water) and, anyway, they and the dog have taken their seasickness pills. Not much later it seems, they're sitting in the stairwell waiting to disembark.

Nobody appears to mind being turfed out of their cabins one hour early…for cleaning.

No Stranger to blue water

'Another Sky' or 'Oh, Monoculture!'

There is another sky Emily Dickinson.

'There is another sky, ever serene and fair,

And there is another sunshine…

..Never mind silent fields…

Here is the brighter garden

Where not a frost has been…'.

Never mind that this has been described as the most British of French ports, some might say that the port officials are more French than British-recognisably more serious -and you could say 'po-faced'.

The couple are not put off, checking people entering France or keeping them out, is a serious business now.

Next stop the hotel. This is a functional place, avant-garde and…French. With furniture sparse and severe, it narrowly avoids a feeling of sleeping in the office.

The view from the window is Breton, pointed roofs, slate- hung houses, and a big sky.

Big Sky

The dog, fairly well trained, stands up at the window, listening to the church clock chiming every hour.

But, the couple, and the dog in her basket, eventually sleep well. At breakfast, they marvel at the DIY egg boiler, eggs 'soft boiled'.

Changing into 'pulls marinières'-Breton jumpers -(of course), and with gleaming shoes polished by the polishing machine they're off.

Independently, they've holidayed in France, but now the agenda is different, it's searching for somewhere to live. Their plan to have no plan is a strength, they hope.

They are optimistic.

At first the silence, and monochromatic colours of northern France are restful. Maybe settling here, there will be space to read, garden, write, think, even get to know each other again.. They like to think they are reflective people…generally

… and it's a relief to drive along quiet roads.

'Is there anything behind us?', says the man on the vacant dual carriageway. 'No', says the woman, ' neither behind us, or in front. '

What luxury these empty roads are, no competitive driving yet, no cars as big as tanks, or cars with indicators that don't seem to work. No people who have no idea how to drive.

They, and the roundabouts, come later.

The couple observe isolated farmhouses with numerous outbuildings, square granite houses, dark Gothic churches and unusual plants. The colour green is popular. There are no cars turning outside windows- no screechy tyres or excitable people in headphones.

This flat vegetable growing land extends for many kilometres. This must be a France that changes only with the seasons. For some people it is still the foreign holidaymakers' dream. Peaceful and rural, a comforting sameness about the crops. A 'get away from it all' sort of place.

'Oh, monoculture,' says the man.

He hasn't noticed the sub-tropical plants in Le Jardin Exotique and Botanique.

He reminds the woman that being Cornish, he could be returning to his rural Celtic roots, after all the Cornish and Breton flags are similarly white and black.

'Yes, different design, 'says the woman.

But the man can't make any sense of Celtic, can't find any similarities to either Welsh or Cornish. But he likes the tales of a self-sufficient land, strong cultural identity, a proud people, and…an unpredictable maritime climate.

He explains that, as a child growing up in Cornwall the family considered themselves Cornish, not English.

'People who cross the Tamar still talk about going into England, some Cornish people never go there'.

Perhaps being Breton too, is as much about being Breton as French.

Same colours, different design

It seems true that France is the least crowded of European nations. With hectares of empty space, everyone can live in natural surroundings- country smells and colours, sunsets and dawns.. and if anyone still needs a seawater 'cure' well, there's always thalassotherapy.

But not everyone wants to be on a farm with no neighbours, or no fifteen minute village stop with bars, cafés restaurants and baker.

They like the northern cool gentle air- and there are some cloudless days- but they are searching for clear, bright light and warming sun..

The man says he wants 'to drive south until the butter melts'. The woman ponders on how far this might be.

Driving on, at midday, they stop at a village. This is 'La France Profonde,' inland France, timeless, silent, deserted. Still an old agricultural country.

From here you definitely can't see Paris, as they say. Some would also say there is a bleakness about all this.

There is the predictable sleeping dog stretched out by the church -with its silenced clock: a market Square, empty, shut. Houses shuttered up, inhabitants seem long gone. The couple say you need to have been born to this life to live here. It's no wonder tractors block the streets of cities to get rural France noticed.

For them -well, they're off.

Their' Croque -monsieur' (lunch) in the picnic basket will come in handy…. and the spare fuel.

The road is long, but easy. The kilometres pass quicker than miles. Soon they are by the long ribbon of water that is the Canal du Midi, the plane trees showing them the way to the Mediterranean.

They like the idea of travelling from Sea to Sea.

A bird chimes..

'Arrival,' or A Room with a View.

Arrival R. S. A Thomas.

Not conscious
that you have been seeking
Suddenly
you come upon it

the village…..
with no road out
but the one you came in by.

A bird chimes
from a green tree
the hour that is no hour
you know. The river dawdles
to hold a mirror for you
where you may see yourself
as you are, a traveller
with the moon's halo
above him, whom has arrived
after long journeying where he
began, catching this
one truth by surprise
that there is everything to look forward to.

The first thing they notice about the south is the clear light-no clouds. But, being November, the second thing they notice is the icy cold wind. This is the Tramontane, cousin of the Mistral. The landscape flat, with vines, offers no wind protection. Only rocks, vines and olives seem to manage.

They have been told that someone touched by the wind will lose their marbles. They worry about their sanity.

Why did they expect it to be always hot and sunny? 'There's no perfect climate,' says the man.

Hopefully he is not missing the warm, wet Westcountry of England.

But, the hamlet up ahead looks like respite, on the banks of the Canal du Midi. A place to rest and refresh and …. warm up. They have read that in times past this stop had been a resting place for travellers on the mail barge, from city to coast. Now road and rail networks transport the wheat wine, wool.

The couple begin to feel like real travellers. After all, there is no plan to stay forever, just passing through on the way to new adventures.

The man says that in its time this canal was structural engineering at its best -as important as the Channel Tunnel today.

The Port House

Their stopover at the Port House turns out not to be a stopover, but a four month stay. As they discover, it's a 'Room with a View' sort of place. Everybody, from everywhere, is on the way to somewhere else.

To be multilingual would have helped.

The couple are given a small flat. Le Patron offers to bring a gas heater. Luckily, the top floor is open to the outside air, (no windows), as the heater fills the room with fumes. Best idea to keep warm, wear all your clothes at once.

In winter the canal becomes a linear village. A community of individuals/eccentrics, perhaps on the water or beside it. It's a place for liveaboards on 'péniches' (houseboats), boats with water gypsies, some just plain boats-some home-made, and some with sofas, dining room tables, potted plants and dishwashers. Some with fierce dogs. Goat skin rugs seem fashionable.

The canal and its bank caters for all tastes. There's a bakery barge, a barge selling antiquarian books, a hat museum, (must be needed).

The couple make friends with everyone.

Near Christmas, somebody has a 70th birthday party. Everybody available acts in character. A retired judge proposes the toast, a diplomat makes a diplomatic speech. A famous painter takes the photos, and a chiropractor smiles a healing smile.

The famous painter has painted a special birthday present of plane tree scenes, plane trees wind- blown and bending almost to the ground.

There are many tales to tell in the winter evenings, everyone knows that they will never meet again..

But, the couple wonder if they might find a home here. They explore some permanent features.

There is a Catholic chapel with a resident Curé. His is a solitary job with a congregation like moving scenery. On this Sunday, the woman is surprised to see him begin Mass by starting up a cassette player, while changing into his cassock. This is to be the accompaniment to the hymns. Monsieur Le Curé is in good voice, the woman(as it is only her) not so much.

Fortunately there is no embarrassing one-to-one homily, and it's soon over.

The woman thanks the Curé, very brave.

She meets the man to go to the restaurant by the canal. It's crowded. All the diners eat at one big table. The couple reserve two places.

The man whispers, 'is that person sitting there a dog?'

Well, yes.

They are told that there is an English couple living here. No one knows who they are, or where they come from. They live in the grandest house in the hamlet, a grand mansion of many rooms.

'Perhaps, being English, they prefer to keep themselves to themselves,' says the man.

After several months, the English couple from the big house speak. It seems they have been ocean-going sailors for most of their days and are reluctant to live in the large house. In fact, most of the rooms are closed up, unused.

This English sailor is happiest in his small boat moored on the canal. Here, being by himself is a choice. Most days he is there, sitting and dreaming….

But one day, there's another birthday. It's the ocean -going sailor's. He and his wife are persuaded to be sociable. A lamb roast is organised to be attended by everyone. Here the couple meet the working English Expat group, mainly skilled workers. They are experts on the legendary French bureaucracy… and bureaucrats.

'I neither like them any more nor any less' says the boat craftsman -speaking from his 20 year experience.

They ask Le Patron, hardly the sunniest of characters, what he thinks about 'les étrangers'.

He comments that renovating (rénovation) of old village houses is a good idea; even better when they are re-sold, preferably to a Frenchman!

But working in France as un étranger, requires 'beaucoup de courage. '

The work permit (papers, visas, rules etc) require a French native's ingenuity and persistence.

Converting chateaux, cultivating vines and planting olive groves is only for the brave.

Luckily, the man and woman have no plans to do any of this.

They settle into daily routines-dog walking, shopping, siesta. They get used to the cicadas making their repetitive racket.

Soon it's New Year's Day at the Port House. This turns out to be very congenial.

People staying and people living there already, appear.

On a clear, bright day the man and woman, and all, are served a breakfast of Calvados and croissants on the canal bank. Everybody toasts everybody. Passing bargees wave and call, 'Bonne année!'

A man throws a ball into the canal, the dog, carefully shampooed, jumps in after it. With shampoo rinsed off in the water, the dog retrieves the ball and jumps back on the canal bank.. After a quick whole body shake the New Year's Day grooming is done. Easy.

There is an English resident, well integrated into French ways. She even understands the woman's not so good French. As a special treat, they go to a meeting of the Troisième âge (third age group). The woman is introduced as a special guest.

There is a long lunch, followed by a longer agenda….

There are many minutes to be read, many resolutions to be passed. The woman doesn't understand much, it doesn't seem to matter.

But now it's nearly spring-and the couple's rooms are needed for holiday makers. Time to go. They are ready and hopeful.

The English boatman has heard from the lockeeper, who has heard from the swimming pool man, about a house for sale in a nearby village.

'A Farewell' or 'Not sure about the Health and Safety'.

A Farewell. Tang Variations.

If you return to the mountains and the valleys

You must find beauty in the heights and the depths:

Don't follow the example of the man

Who never travels beyond the peach garden

Where we play.

The Cuckoo Clock House

It's a sort of cuckoo clock house, says the English boatman. At the end of an ´impasse, 'or blind alley- is a garage door.

'Is this it?' says the woman.

The garage houses a freestanding retro bath with 'very nice' tiling.

'This could make a self-contained apartment, 'says the helpful estate agent.

The next floor is a sitting room, a corner kitchen, and best of all they are told, a log burner. It gets very cold here in winter. (difficult to imagine in 30°C).

The mezzanine floor-a balcony with bedrooms-is also a good place for growing giant cactus. And then….. there's the courtyard, accessible via the street. Here is a very tall banana tree and a fig. Impressively, the well is working too. Not sure about the mosquitoes.

They love it all.

A few weeks later, with the help of the boatman, they move in, the boatman's boat used as a very large suitcase.

Life here they find, is lived very slowly. The main events are the pizza van, selling fruit pizzas cooked over souches (vine roots) in the van, and the weekly market.

'It will be in its usual place', says the loudspeaker.. (where is that?)

There is a brisk trade in overalls and slippers. 'All you need to live here. ' says the neighbour.

Otherwise, the neighbours, although mainly taciturn, are the main source of information. First, the couple have to submit to the two metre stare. A sort of determined noticing. There is the residents petition: the air-conditioning unit at the village shop is too noisy and should be removed. (the couple sign it).

…And then there is the dog warden who takes his job very seriously indeed. The dog is given a warning.

The best thing about this village for them is its' position above the floodplain, it doesn't flood.

The couple say, 'Well, it's a start !'

They know that to get on, understand, and make things work in a country where English is not the first language, requires hard work and diligence. The woman thinks she has those qualities 'in spades', the man isn't so motivated.

In this, some would say, insular, inland French village there are few foreign voices. The couple are expected to speak understandable French -and people will wait until they do. The woman tries hers at the Pharmacy. She stutters a bit. The assistant is unmoved.

'Comment ?'Quoi?'(here used as what?) Franglais is not acceptable.

The assistant asks her to speak French. The woman taken off-guard and feeling helpless says

'Why don't you try English?'

Temporarily she feels better, but she still leaves the shop empty-handed. The man says, rather than take offence, play for time.

Try 'Ooh Là!, and 'Bien sûr'.

But perhaps there is help somewhere as things soon change.

They are told that there is a famous English doctor living in the village, who each week presides over the Salon, (French conversation class) He is spoken of with reverence, - 'some people have been fortunate to be in his presence.' The woman is invited.

This is to be a testing experience.

As a preliminary, the woman is asked to read some French texts to the group-and then politely, asked to listen to the difference when a French person reads them. Oh dear.

She is chastened when one German member gets up and leaves saying, 'I have learned nothing today'. It seems that today, the French out-German the German in linguistic skills.

Is it always like this?

But the coffee is aromatic and strong, and the important doctor and his wife become friends.

After a while, the family are curious to see how the man, woman and dog are getting on.

A French get-together is organised. The family come by plane, rail and ship.

The first day is Mediterranean hot, over 30°C.

The local baker arrives, holding shoulder high a giant pizza, enough for a crowd.

The barbecued lamb is stupendous. Everyone has a go at

speaking French.

The next day, the family are taken to the local (only) village restaurant. 'Not sure about the Health and Safety there,' says the famous doctor. The family are asked to dress up and to prepare themselves for a French dining experience.

On a ferociously hot day, down a very hot side street, behind a small door in a private house is the restaurant.

The friendly owner, elderly, in overalls and probably slippers, shows them to a long table. There seems to be a party going on somewhere.

Endless courses are served from a kind of school dinner trolley. Nobody recognises the meat, but it tastes fine.

Eventually coffee arrives in an enamel teapot. They join in the 'Hokey Cokey' procession from the party.

'What an experience!' say the family.

Some days later, the sleepy village starts to come to life, posters appear. There is to be a special 10 year celebration- the 'Fête de Vendanges.'

The Procession

This is no ordinary harvest festival, this is a celebration of the vine, the vineyards, les vignerons, and wine. Attendance at this festival is mandatory for all the traditionalists.

On the day, wine pours from the fountain, chestnuts are roasting in a huge, spinning barrel, rhythmic marching bands are marching, the drumming hypnotic. Oxen are driven down the narrow streets. The village is transformed. Every living soul left in the village is now out, drinking, eating or clapping. The elderly neighbour is dancing as if his shoes are on fire!

The church doors are wide open, the wine processed to the church to be blessed along with everyone else. Even the famous doctor, in traditional costume, is driven in the procession in the chief vigneron's vintage car….

They can see why people are happy and proud living in their community, but the couple are not part of it. it's great to be outsiders, and not bother with   local gossip or politics, but living inland is much too hot. No coastal breezes either.

The man comments,

'Have you noticed the name of the next street, translated, means the street of the hot oven?'

In no time, they sell the cuckoo clock house, (to someone who likes the self-contained apartment in the garage.)

'Desiderata' Max Ehrmann, or Back to Base.

Desiderata Max Ehrmann

..Enjoy your achievements as well as your plans.

Keep interested in your own career,

however humble,

it is a real possession in the changing fortunes of time…

The Woman has been a career girl for most of her life. Her family are used to the odd hours of healthcare, call-outs and concerns. But now... the family has their own family, their own independence and careers -and are busy.

She think she might like to reconnect with her working past and see the family too (if they have time!).

Four meetings a year as a Trustee will use her old skills and keep her brain up to date. How rusty is her English?

This time crossing the English channel is not in a cruise ship- just a superfast train, and she can stop off in 'The City of Light'.

Arriving from a pied-à-terre in Paris, does have a certain cachet.

The meeting starts. She hopes she is not back in the world of status and hierarchies. The woman finds that her English, as she feared, is not that good. How can she' hit the ground running, 'think outside the box' or try 'blue sky thinking?'.

How does she concentrate in 'the attention economy?'. Surreptitiously, she searches for a glossary.

But it is congenial, considerate and relaxed. After a good lunch including tapenade, (ground olives) as a nod to the Englishwoman, she is at least partly functioning. She begins to sympathise with and understand her French counterparts who struggle with rules, formats, codes. No relaxing allowed for them.

After the meeting there are English bookshops to visit, walks in the park and afternoon tea. But everybody except her is in a tearing hurry, traffic deafening, normal conversation silenced as pedestrians walk -eyes dangerously glued- to mobile phones. How is it they don't walk into each other?

Although she doesn't really mind the drizzle…and the wet pavements -and everywhere mottled with rain, she thinks about the quiet sunlit days she has left behind..

Meanwhile, the man is pondering on how to bring his sailing boat from England.

Sea Fever John Masefield, or 'This boat has a value y'know'.

Sea Fever.

I must go down to the seas again, to the lonely sea and sky.
And all I ask is a tall ship and a star to steer her by;

And the wheel's kick and the wind's song and the white sails shaking.

And a grey mist on the sea's face and a grey dawn breaking.

I must go down to the seas again, for the call of the running tide

Is a wild call and a clear call that may not be denied: And all I ask is a windy day with the white clouds flying,

And the flung spray and the blown spume and the sea-gulls flying.

I must go down to the seas again, to the vagrant gypsy life,

To the gull's way and the whale's way where the wind's like a whetted knife;

And all I ask is a merry yarn from a laughing fellow-rover,

And quiet sleep and a sweet dream when the long trick's over.

The Seafarer

From childhood, the man has always loved the sea. His mother had loved the sea too, although her favourite expression was 'worse things happen at sea. ' She used to sit on a rock until 'the last tide went out. '

He has the Westcountryman's combination of fear and excitement about sailing -and water. A wooden boat is a place to tinker and feel he can take off, if life is getting just too much. The man organises a trip to get the boat from England to a small inland French port. An English Channel trip with an experienced crew -then a relaxing meander down inland French waterways. That is the plan.

After negotiating a fast flowing and dangerous river Garonne- and then into the canal system-it's a relief to arrive at the peaceful Canal du Midi. With the railway line and train (TGV) running alongside, the laptop toilers wave from the windows.

In the French port are experts-shipwrights, boatbuilders, ex-coast guards who work with wood. All have served their apprenticeships in boat yards.

Boat language is universal.

The man, being the wise type, is allowed to join the group. Mediterranean weather conditions have to be studied: the sea looks calm enough, but what about the wind? Are there gales? The most dangerous thing is the sun pounding down.

Hot sun on wood is a new feature.

The experts know all the answers or know someone who does. The working day here is relaxed. 'No work when it's windy,' says the Frenchman, 'and long lunches, 12-5 pm. '

The ex -coast guard, a sociable sort, invites anyone he can see to lunch -in any language he can think of.

'But you can't cook Richard,' says his wife. Answer -'Oh no, I can't, can I ?'

Never mind, try the Traiteur

Le Déjeuner

The man hopes to have his boat name smartened up. The signwriter is coming-'definitely' -but then is delayed due to 'cool' weather. The paint won't dry (of course).

But the English boat craftsman is the reliable best, he can make wood talk, they say.

He says, 'this boat has a value y'know.'

A marina and mooring is the next stop. The man books his place on the coast. It's not available when he arrives in his boat.

'Pas possible, ' says the Capitainerie, Oh…

After complicated manoeuvering, the man makes the ex-coastguard a part owner-and moves the boat into his space.

The wooden boat on its mooring looks spectacular, it's name and polished wood gleaming, even though the sign writer never returned.

The youngest son comes to stay-new to boats then, but keen, he is given a tour. The man plays his jazz CDs. Next time a 'trip out' he says 'just as soon as I can find an experienced crew. '

The short stayers on the marina, known only by their boat names, do not seem interested in making friends. En route to somewhere else, their interests are mainly where to eat and drink, maybe a brief discussion about the problems with the euro exchange rate, then a cursory look around and on. They say this is 'living the dream'. But the long-stayers are usually lifelong boat people, swapping yarns, adventure stories, real, or imaginary, many live nearby.

Some boats never move.

One day, the oldest son comes, a handy sort of person, and the man ventures 'out'. Unusually there is no wind. 'Can we go any faster do you think?' Motor fires up, it is a motor -sailor after all.

Going out'

Or perhaps they prefer fishing-and a day of heat and silence.

As time goes on, the wooden boat turns into a full-time job. There is the hauling out by a crane, the scraping off of shellfish, the anti fouling -and of course- the varnishing in the hot sun. Never mind the decks cracking.

And all has to be done early in the morning. 'This is why there are no wooden boats here, or 'woodies'. (boat enthusiasts.) says the man.

The experts gradually thin out and aren't replaced. Only the local fishermen are interested in wooden boats; the romance of the sea, being sent off to sleep by the comforting creak.

Sadly this wooden retreat has to go.

The man, woman and dog have bigger fish to fry.

Afternoon on a hill, or The Enchantment

Afternoon on a Hill, Edna St Vincent Millay.

I will be the gladdest thing

Under the sun!

I will touch a hundred flowers

And not pick one.

I will look at cliffs and clouds

With quiet eyes,

Watch the wind bow down the grass,

And the grass rise

And when lights begin to show

Up from the town,

I will mark which must be mine,

And then start down!

It's spring now, so the man woman and dog turn their faces to the sun and head south, towards the coast.

Unlike the famous doctor in the inland village ('You're not coastal are you!'), they are coastal people, grown up with the sound of the sea and the cry of the seabirds.

The man says his favourite word is beach.

Their spirits lift as the weather warms up -and the sea is enclosed in the rocky Mediterranean shoreline. The landscape is now olive trees, vines and pines. There are tracts of vineyards, the colours are softer, the air smells of thyme and rosemary.

In the clear light, the blue sky seems even bluer. Even the dog looks out of the car window. The couple are searching for a home. This will probably not be an old ornate French house, or something in a concrete tower block, or modern, on a lotissement (estate).

Along the south coast road they call at 'Immobiliers' (estate agents). They are told there is an interesting village ahead.

The agent describing it, artfully says, 'Can you hear the sun in my voice?'

A good selling point.

This village used to be nearly completely surrounded by water, almost an island, an area of land surrounded by sea on three sides. The sea has receded, leaving étangs. Fishermen who live here have stayed: houses have been passed down the generations. It is rare to find one for sale, and if it is- then multiple renovation is often required. The exchange of property is not of much interest. Some of the houses look abandoned.

The grandest buildings, sometimes four storeys high, once belonged to salt traders. Now, most of the village is built in a circle around what was a look-out tower used as refuge in case of pirate invasion.

A sort of semi-island paranoia.

Most of these homes had interconnecting doors in the lofts(to get away from pirates.) Some 14 families still live here, families have intermarried, some left and returned. The couple are told poetically that they will be 'seduced by the blue sea, the étangs and hills at night, when the mystery of the village will enchant them'.

'Ici, le parler, le sourire, vous séduiront et vous accorderont avec le bleu de la mer, des étangs des collines, au soir tout ce que le mystère de …. vous aura dérobé'.   Claude Gerini.

They understand from the immobilier that the purchase of a house is a no going back procedure. It involves a legal framework from beginning to end drawn up by a government officer, called a 'Notaire' respectfully known as Maître.

The Notaire

Once over the first 'interest in buying' period the 'Compromis de Vente,' big penalties ensure that the buyer doesn't change his mind. The couple take along the French neighbour in case of misunderstandings. She seems nervous. They note that the estate agent is now wearing a complicated looking hat, not her usual beach straw. The gold plated icon of the French Republic on the door, gives them a clue of what to expect.

Introduced to a polite, unsmiling man, the Mâitre, they follow him into an interior office with leather padded chairs and a large desk. Secretaries are on guard outside.

After long shuffling of paper and throat clearing, the business begins. The buyer's representative, (the helpful neighbour), is silent. They listen as details of their marital status, names of children, jobs, places and dates of birth(surely they aren't as old as that?) are read out. Then there is the same embarrassment for the sellers. (The neighbour whispers it's about fraud.)

Just when they appear to be getting somewhere, the helpful neighbour raises her hand. They wait.

'What about the swamp?' she says. 'Swamp' to rhyme with 'lamp. '

The swamp? Aah, this needs looking into. The couple are worried. Is the house built on a floodplain? Will the garden soon be a swimming pool? Secretaries are sent for, land registry checked, riverbeds studied. It seems that this house is unlikely to be flooded, the Mediterranean has receded, despite the dire warnings of global warming.

They individually, initial each page of the 20 page document, and thankfully leave.

The house they buy is a fisherman's house facing water. It has a bisque coloured facade and red clay roof tiles. From here they can smell the sea, the view is perfect, they can watch the flamingos.

One entrance is in the village street, where neighbours sit on window ledges (anyone's) and chat. Being English, the couple put flowers on theirs.

A place to chat

The other entrance is into a courtyard-concrete -with boots and fishing nets still there.

Blue Water laid out in front of them…

In the house there are generations of furniture, china and even clothes. 'When is the removal van coming?' asks the woman.

Silly question.

They clear it with enthusiasm. It has a' Belle Époque ' feel about it with chandeliers, heavy dark wood furniture and very sombre marble.. Do they want it to be like everyone else's

-square with walls painted white, and tasteful graphite coloured shutters?

Perhaps a facade of rough stone -as a weather screen.

Blue water is laid out in front of them, so maybe look right through to it with an uncluttered empty cool space.

It is a house of fresh air.

Narrow Road to the Deep North. Bashō, translated by Nobuyuki Yuasa..

I felt quite at home….

Sleeping lazily

In this house of fresh air.

In the utter silence

Of a temple,

A cicada's voice alone

Penetrates the rocks…

The woman wonders if she might like some shady dark corners.

While thinking about this the man is pondering on a garden. For most people here, any outside space is a car park, or very possibly a swimming pool. But they haven't come here to swim lengths. They like the long quiet beaches and would prefer to swim in the bath -warm (usually) water of the Mediterranean Sea. It's outside their gate.

A kind of garden is possible, if at the moment it is full of rubble, rocks and very, very dry soil.

'Dust and stones,' says the man.

Importing soil is difficult. The blustery wind blows away the topsoil. The neighbour, who says she is not 'temperamentally suited 'to gardening, comes to look.

'An English garden,' she says.

Not really, (no lawn, no rockery, no herbaceous borders.) The man draws a plan of curves and bends. This is not to be a perfectly maintained, parterre and topiary, He can plant things that are beautiful, not because he needs to eat them. He learns to use plants and trees that grow wild-rosemary, vines, olives, possibly a lemon tree.

'We like different shades of green, they say…very restful. ' They add a bronze heron, some terracotta latticed wind breaks, a mirror- and it is done. The garden is an oasis, shady and quiet.

A granddaughter comes 'Where are all the people?' she says.

The cyprus and umbrella pine they plant grow and grow. They have to take advice from La Marie(town hall) as the trees begin to obliterate the sky.

The history of this village, isolated by water, is partly linked to the precarious and dangerous lives of the fishermen. With a mix of superstition, religion and reality, the older citizens('Les Anciens,') tell tales of the men lost at sea. Catholicism here is deeply rooted in local activities and celebrations.

The neighbour has history in this village. He says, 'we must teach our children about our traditions', and, 'I expect to live a long time, as old people here are pickled in salt!'

Although fishing is a small industry now, mainly supplying a fish quay and the local restaurants, the spirit of the past is kept alive by the fishermen's descendants.

In the ornate church with its plaster saints and gold leaf covered ceiling, St Peter, the fishermen's patron saint and protector, stands desolately by a shipwreck.

In midsummer, a statue of the Saint is processed to the Church and through the village. Lead by the Mayor and the town band, the voices of all generations mournfully chant their hymn- to please the Saint.

The chorus, repeated over and over has been said to weave a kind of enchantment. The woman observes that the man, even with a scientists' scepticism, pauses to say a little prayer asking for protection.

St. Pierre. A kind of Enchantment.

Saint Pierre Hymne.

Ho, Saint Pierre, pour te plaire, je veux marcher sous ton drapeau
(To please you Saint Pierre I want to walk under your flag)

'I taught myself to live simply' or 'What do you do all day, sunbathe?'

I taught myself to live simply, Anna Akhmatova

I taught myself to live simply and wisely, to look at the sky ….

. and to wander long before evening to tire my superfluous worries.

…I come back. The fluffy cat licks my palm, purrs so sweetly and the fire flares bright…

... Only the cry of a stork landing on the roof occasionally breaks the silence.

If you knock on my door I may not even hear.

The couple begin to live a French life. This means doing what the locals do. They have yet to meet the stereotypical Frenchman, in a beret, a dog-end in his mouth, complaining about his liver. Politics is not an interest either, except to say that the President (every President) is a joke, une blague.

The Midi is seen as different from the rest of France, more relaxed, different language. Some people speak Occitan. They say they live simply.

The retired people seem to appreciate living in a rural paradise. Not full of noise, they say.

The neighbours would like to know the couple better.

What do they like about being here, are they beginning to fit in, what about the language?

Having heard 2 year olds in the street speaking perfect French - and being thoughtfully corrected by their parents('it's chevaux, ma chérie pas cheval') the woman asks what her accent sounds like to French ears. She has been practising. 'You speak very carefully, and pronounce every syllable' she is tactfully told.

Could be worse.

The couple expect the Mediterranean weather to be hot sun, all day, every day, especially in winter. They are envied by English acquaintances,

'bet you won't miss the rainy English winters'.

Their experience is not what they expected.

'There is no perfect climate, ' says the man.

To understand the weather, the neighbours tell them, start with the Pyrenees mountains and Massif Central. This is where the winds blow from. They can be frequent, especially in winter.

Driving south on the Spanish road, they notice that the 'snow-capped'. Pyrenees seem to stay snow-capped into summer. No wonder their uninterrupted view of water can bring frequent icy blasts.

'Can you assure me that this wind won't blow every day? ' says an English client to the Immobilier. Very difficult. The neighbour has a different view.

'C'est frais, '(fresh) he says. 'On respire, '(we can breathe). Hmmm.

Otherwise, it's sunny and hot, little rain and some spectacular, even frightening, thunderstorms. The weather pattern has no pattern so it's difficult to predict.

Life in the Midi is lived mainly according to this weather. So, for half the year there is brilliant sunshine, bright blue skies.. They become used to the hot white light of summer.

And, for the other half, it's still clear sparkly light, blue skies, but … wind.

The villagers pay close attention to the weather. Very hot is regarded as 'tiède'(tepid, luke-warm,) and the wind has a purpose, it blows away clouds and mosquitoes. Only the warm wet 'Marin' from the south east is unpopular. It brings cloud and, rarely, rain.

Just like Angleterre it is said.

Village life for them is a leisurely affair. The day begins with a baguette. The most popular person in the village is the artisan baker. Daily, the patient baguette queue extends down the street. There are 8 types of bread. The patisserie, created every day, is an art form.

The master baker is up at 4 am.

The woman loves the bite size concoctions: she watches carefully as a tiny bird -like lady in minuscule jeans passes, eating her way through a selection of patisserie. No calorie counting involved.

There is only one difficulty. The mainly teenage staff, 'les ados', are apparently like the Parisian waiters, impoli (rude). The couple certainly don't get' service with a smile'. What a let-down for the hard-working baker.

The first village sounds are the whirring brushes of the street cleaning machine, a waft of detergent drifts in the window- with their first cup of coffee. Then, it's the dog mess motorbike vacuum cleaner.

With their first bite of baguette, it's the follow -up street cleaning men with their trolleys and brushes. They joke that if they can't manage street cleaning there's always grape picking.

Later, the cleaners will take their break and stretch out under the lime trees.

The gardeners are next, pruning lopping and tidying. Last call are the bin men, bins emptied every day. This is a hot country.

In response to the weather or personal mood -the village shops open -and close. Sometimes they will re-open on a particular Saints Day if only the shopkeeper could remember when that is.

The rhythm of village days is unchanging. The market shopping is thoughtful, melons examined and sniffed, morsels of bread tasted. Whether the market is big or small, the displays of seasonal produce are a masterclass in presentation -and it all has to be cleared away by 1 pm

It's ok says the stall holder- 'we have every afternoon off. '

Masterclass.

Market Shopping

The woman gets to see regular traders, they like to joke with her, usually about their favourite topic, the weather. 'The sun will be out later 'they say, or, 'it's spring this morning and summer this afternoon. '

Today, she has a question. Speaking to the proprietor of an elegantly arranged clothes stall, almost like a boutique, she comments, 'All your clothes are 'jolies couleurs' no black, navy, beige. Who do you sell them to?'

'People like you Madame. '

Much time every day is taken up with discussing the next meal. By midday the cafe street tables are busy, a message of 'let's take a break and eat. '

'Moules frites' (mussels and chips) is the favourite.

These village meals are sociable affairs, long and congenial, talking is expected and conversation buzzes. People are together with a common enthusiasm-eating, talking and food. Most days, at midday (and evening too), the street eating experience can be seen, smelt and heard. It's not surprising that there's not often grazing in the street, who would want to spoil their appetite?

In fact the local supermarket advises against it...' Èvitez de grignoter entre les repas.' (don't snack between meals.)

Although the man and woman agree that the Mediterranean diet has health benefits, in other ways they differ. He is a self - indulgent gourmand (greedy) meat eater, she a discerning gourmet (she says) with a liking for fish, definitely more suited to a fishing village.

Like their neighbours, neither of them see food as part of a slimming diet, un régime, but more a part of enjoying life, a form of relaxation.

They have a favourite restaurant, five minutes away.

Similar to much of the property in the village, this restaurant is a converted fisherman's house. Built to be cool, with an overhanging vine and fig in a courtyard, it usually has tables pushed together to make one long one. Guests often come in twelves. Eating here is less about gastronomy and more about conviviality.

Today the youngest son has come to stay - so they are three.

La Patronne, who knows the couple, politely nods a greeting. Typical food does not necessarily involve lobsters, fish and oysters, although it might.

Impressively the youngest son makes some adventurous choices. 'Yes, we probably all like squid?' Immediately the bread arrives, no French table must be without bread, a carafe of tap water, and of course, food artfully arranged.

All ages are dressed for the serious business of eating. The smallest child in the room has on couture shorts. It is said that the French claim to cut jeans better than anyone else. This seems right. The very slim elderly man at the next table has ironed jeans suspended on tiny hips -by smart red braces.

Everyday clothes here are smart, matching and stylish, no polyester sandals. The youngest son, a confident traveller, has luckily brought his dining out gear. Quiet conversation fills the room, everyone expansive -and the squid is perfectly cooked. The youngest son smiles. The couple are pleased, it is an occasion. Perhaps the Sunday visit to the restaurant is the high point of the week. An orderly queue forms to pay, as the clock in the Square chimes two o'clock. There are general 'au revoirs' said into the room. The couple say a special 'au revoir' to their neighbouring diner, the very slim elderly man, before retiring for a siesta.

Le repas dans la rue, or 'someone.'

In this village community loyalties are first to the family, secondly to the people next door or opposite -and then to the nearby neighbours. This is ' Le Quartier. ' If people move from one street to the next, they are welcomed to the new Quartier.

Now it is midsummer and there is the special' repas dans la rue'(street meal.)This is rather an exclusive affair. To be invited you must be a full member of the street, no passers -by allowed. No residents from the next street. In fact if you gatecrash you will be asked to leave.

This is a Mairie authorised meal, the street is closed, the fairy lights are put up, there is a stern no parking notice on a notice board.

'Someone', the same person every year -appears. They collect the money, do the shopping, set out tables and do the cooking. Every year it's the same, a fish and chicken sort of paella cooked in a large cauldron in the street. It all starts quietly and then gets really loud. 'Barcelona' (not that far away after all) is bashed out, nobody knows the words. Les Anglais are asked to sing. 'Where is your 'esprit ?' they say, as the couple stammer and cringe.

The cooks' teenage son, carefully trying a bit of English, says 'everyone will be hammered by midnight!'

At midnight, not 'hammered' but cheerful, the party disbands. The next day there will be no trace of it, magically cleared away, by' someone'.

The next day, with the sun directly overhead and it's scorching, everyone heads indoors. Siesta means closed shutters and windows, silent streets, closed shops and hush. It is peaceful. Time ticks past, traffic at a standstill. The dog sleeps in her basket…

Even later, doors open and the neighbours appear with chairs, to sit under the lime tree. Conversations catch up from the day before. This is a sort of 'assisted living;' there is always someone who knows where to buy a mouse trap, or can supply you with fennel(to eat with the fish, naturally.) They soon fall into the perfect rhythm of talk and silence on a long summer evening.

Sometimes the woman joins them. They like the story of the teenager who came to stay, the one who crept into the couples ' kitchen late at night to get a sneaky glass or two of 'vin ordinaire' and, embarrassingly, bumped into the woman.

'Anglais?' they ask. The woman nods.

'Mal élevé Madame' they say, sympathetically.

Midsummer evenings are a luxury, predictably warm. Village shops stay open until the last customer goes home, and the holiday makers talk and eat late into the night.

This is just to say. William Carlos Williams.

This is just to say

I have eaten

the plums

that were in the ice box

and which you were probably saving

for breakfast.

Forgive me

they were delicious

so sweet

and so cold.

'I started early'. Emily Dickinson.

I started Early-Took my Dog-

And visited the Sea-

The Mermaids in the Basement

Came out to look at me-

Sometimes, before the big heat, the couple pack their parasol and head for one of the long white beaches. The dog doesn't come, the sand seems to be too hot for paws.

Getting a sun tan is not a priority, but listening to the calming sound of the waves, is. The water is usually warm, salty and buoyant-flat calm and easy to potter in. The neighbour potters past, in the water, matching swimsuit and jewellery. Her friends murmur along beside her.

The woman doesn't need the library books in the beach library.

The beach library

There is a routine to the day.

Eating is not part of this, unpacking picnic boxes is not usual. As it gets near midday, it's time to leave for 'une salade' and a siesta in the shade.

'And whatever your labours and aspirations, in the noisy confusion of life, keep peace in your soul. '
Desiderata. Max Ehrmann.

The Healer, (part 1.)

The couple haven't seen a friend from the next street for some while. She is known as the village healer. Her house shutters are closed, the special bird bath has not been replenished, or the drinking water for passing cats, dogs - and seagulls. A familiar sight, she can usually be seen just looking, standing, or chatting in the street. Where is she? The neighbours haven't seen her either. The couple are worried. They tap on her door. She has a problem with her eye and is 'resting.'

The woman, being an ex health professional, is concerned. Seen a doctor, an ophthalmologist perhaps?

Maybe urgent.

The healer is unimpressed. How is her vision? No vision.

Panicking, the woman offers to drive her to the hospital.

The Healer is relaxed, not convenient at the moment, I have my tax forms to do. Perhaps later?

Oh well….

The Healer, (part 2.)

The man has a problem with his wrist, maybe it's premature ageing. He mentions it to the healer. This lady has status in the village, she has 'special powers' he is told.

An appointment in the street(better light) is made. The healer reappears, surprisingly now wearing a white coat and carrying a black bag. The man sits on a doorstep and attention is given to the wrist, hand and arm.

'How are the fingers?'(fine.)

'What about raising the arm ?'(ok.) 'Can he write?'(he is right - handed).

After careful consideration and some laying on of hands, the healer presents her plan.

'Go home now'.

The man expects to go to the Pharmacy. No, that is not it.

'Go home and take a photo of your wrist, then I can work on it from here. '

She does healing at a distance too.

The man recounts the tale to the woman.

'Oh well, it can't do any harm can it?' she says.

Best to stay on good terms with the neighbours

The neighbour opposite lives alone, mainly in an upstairs room, she prefers it that way. From time to time, feeling sociable, she puts a towel on her widow as a signal to chat. She calls to the woman. 'Tu veux danser?' As regards her health, well, she may be ill, but 'hospitals are places that make you ill. Attention at home is best. Anyway, it is possible to be cured twice as fast at home as in hospital' she says.

The 'singing man' says 'Bonjour, ' most days. He is an eccentric- slightly off balance somehow, but a happy man. He has found a way of life in this village that he likes. This is not about just shambling around. He has a repertoire of songs, all stored in his head. Arms outstretched, he sings to the captive audience outside the Bar. They lean back and enjoy it. Some even clap. He recognises the woman and speaks to her dog.

'I will hold her for you. '

The man takes the lead. He seems to be walking off with the dog.

'Don't worry' she says, hastily taking the dog back, 'Perhaps a walk another day. '

Walking in the street, the English woman hears a bicycle bell. It is the village musician, a talented saxophonist.

'Ça Va?' Do the English like it here?(Yes)

Do they still only eat 'le pain de mie' in England?(sliced white bread). (No)

He is happier asking questions than answering them.

He calls out to friends, stopping for a chat, then home for a bit of music-maybe a little déjeuner léger '-and 'un peu de soleil'(not too much.) He is content.

Best to stay on good terms with the neighbours.

The airport run.

Today, the eldest son is arriving. It is a day of baking Mediterranean heat, almost like North Africa, but we know he loves it..

The woman drives for an hour or two to the airport, car air-conditioning overwhelmed. The road to the airport is not signed. She ends up in a large town searching. It is siesta time. The only inhabitant still awake can't remember the way, but helpfully offers suggestions. By chance, the woman spots a tiny pictogram of an aeroplane on a roundabout. She thanks the man, then follows the direction on the roundabout. One hour later she pulls into the car park. The plane is on the tarmac and the doors are opening. The eldest son is beaming. He is a little overdressed in anorak, trainers, socks and heavy duty denim jeans. Luckily, his south of France wardrobe is in the woman's house (still there from last time.)There are smiles all round and enthusiastic jumping from the dog.

The Little Theatre

Against this backdrop of blue skies and warm days, the man and woman can't imagine how anything can get even better.

Today there is an air of suppressed excitement. It's the opening night of the little theatre. The man finds a poster on a drain pipe, start time, 8 pm.

Arriving early, (perhaps a crowd is expected,) there is already a queue outside a small door in a village house.

At 8 pm exactly, a dinner jacketed man, with bare feet, opens the door.

'Madame, Monsieur, le théâtre est ouvert. '

It is dark inside, so

'just sit down' says the man.

'The woman looks around nervously. Where are the fire exits? No fire exits.

A ticking metronome is the only thing visible. It seems to be counting down to something. Of course -'Les Artistes.' Two village musicians appear. In subdued lighting they start their repertoire, the woman on piano, the man saxophone. It is the famous saxophonist. This is a rendition of Gershwin's summertime they have never heard before… The soprano voice soars and swoops.

The evening continues -with more of the same. It could be called modern, or perhaps, experimental.

'Anyone have the time ?' asks the saxophonist, after several hours.

Around midnight, after various intervals, it is probably the finale.

'Encore!' calls the audience.

At 1am, the couple tumble out into the street. This village is certainly not a cultural desert.

The Choir

It is unusual to have a mix of culture and beach, usually it's one or the other.

Music and theatre play a big part in village life. There are the concerts in the Square(la place), sea shanty singers in the street, big bands and modern jazz. With a background of heat, everything is 'en plein air.'

And then there's the choir…..

One evening the woman goes with Mireille to a choir rehearsal. She notes that Mireille is wearing a very smart dress and, not unsurprisingly, stands in the front row, hands carefully clasped in front of her. The woman looks for a place of obscurity. Try the back row. The choir mistress arrives, exactly on time. She taps her foot twice and magically there is a silence-followed by the first notes from the women's group, the 'altos'. The choir mistress looks around. The woman's throat feels parched as she notices the choir lady leaning in, listening to her. Better just mouth the words. But then, the male voices are brought in- bass and tenor-miraculous, the air vibrates, even the woman can sing well now. Soon they are rocking!

As suddenly as it started the evening is over with another tap of the foot.

Music is collected up. 'Well done everybody. See you next week?'

A tea party

Children have a special place in everyone's hearts in the village. The grandmother opposite is making a rare appearance, fully dressed, to see her grandchildren.

The village school organises complicated outings to include healthy, teacher-led walks or maybe all out on scooters.

The children's school meals menus are posted weekly on the Mairie notice board, 'bio '(organic)of course-even the fish and chips.

Menu Scolaire

The French neighbour must be the only French woman in the village who drinks tea. Not the' lavender scented' tisane type, but black assam tea. She draws the line at sugar and milk.

The woman is invited to tea to meet 'les jeunes'(young people.)

Aurélie and Inès meet her at the door, ages 14 and 10.

Tea is set out formally on the table, quite a ceremony, with porcelain cups and saucers- and panettone- a kind of Italian bread.

Conversation is to be mainly in English. The neighbour has lived in America. She asks ' How is the dog, is she having a ' lay on?' The woman politely explains' it's lie in '.

This language thing is difficult!

Aurélie goes to fetch her English homework(about describing a trip to London), Inès opens her case of maquillage (make- up) and demonstrates her skills as a future esthécienne. I may need a Diploma for this, she says. The woman chooses mauve eyeshadow, definitely an improvement.

Aurélie talks about school, the teachers(moyen, average) the friends(très bien, very good)learning a language(difficile), the courses(all about Diplomas.)'

'How is she getting on with English?'

If you want to know what's going on in the world you can't speak only French, says her mother.

Aurélie prefers German.

The interior of this house is a showpiece of good taste and thoughtful lakeside building. A huge window, maximising the view, turns the outside lake into an infinity pool. The internal spiral staircase, reminding her of the Tate Modern, goes skywards. The courtyard is tastefully planted with grasses.

The woman does her best with the English homework and leaves. Later she has a message from Inès thanking her for 'helping her to understand English.' She is impressed.

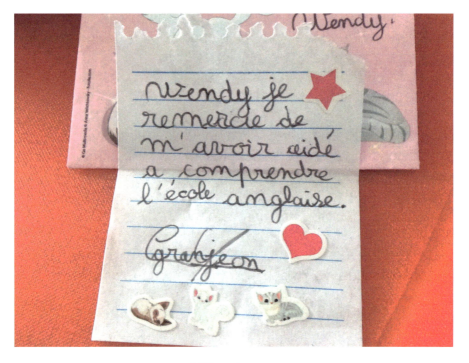

A Thank you

Cartoon books known as les 'bandes dessinées', are popular not only with children, but with all ages. There is a yearly village exhibition of books, some of them rare first editions.

The most well known, the Franco -Belgian Tintin and the French Astérix and Obelix, are thought by the French to represent aspects of their personalities.

Tintin, a roving reporter, defends injustice, Astérix, a tactical warrior, is shrewd and intelligent. His slower thinking friend Obelix may be corpulent and food obsessed, but he is super strong.

Every story ends with a banquet, naturally.

'The purpose of life is not to get bored' (Levi-Strauss).

In this child -centred, progressive village it seems unbelievable that any 'jeune' could be bored.

Today the village square has life sized board games (bagatelle, draughts.) A giant hopscotch court is drawn on the ground by a cheerful looking 'games supervisor' in a pointy elf hat.

A carousel whizzes round, a balloon man cycles past handing out free balloons -and the street musicians sashay down the street. The walking tree figures playing violin and accordion don't frighten anyone.

The Tree Musicians

And yet…

L' été, or the bored schoolboy. (I am bored, Je m'ennuie)

The long, hot days of the Mediterranean summer have arrived. The school children are ready and excited by the free days ahead, all except Henri.

Henri, just turned 12 years old, has a new 'Hawaiian' shirt, new tortoiseshell glasses and a very smart cool haircut. His father is skateboarding and go - karting down the street, his mother, a powerful swimmer, is on the beach. There is endless sunshine, blue skies, but…there is a problem,

'Je m'ennuie,' he sighs.

'Lost in translation.'

It's midsummer, the house is warming, it's very hot.

'Try replacing the chandeliers with cooling ceiling fans' says a friend.

The woman has seen a van with 'entre mer and

garrigue'(between sea and scrubland,)In small print it also says, 'électricien.'

She rings the number, leaves a message. He will get back to her.

Sometime later there is a crashing knock on the door. A man with a puce face and tool kit and- in a hurry -is ready to start.

The woman shows him the chandeliers. There are several; perhaps he could start with replacing one, but be sure to leave the one in the salon.

The électricien only speaks Occitan(she doesn't), but after careful explanation he nods and is left to get on with it.

Dashing in from the van he starts taking down the nearest chandelier. It is done in no time and a new fan put up.

It's just a pity it's the wrong one. it's the one in the salon.

He takes it down and starts again..

Leisure. W. H. Davies.

What is this life if, full of care,
We have no time to stand and stare?

No time to stand beneath the boughs,
And stare as long as sheep and cows:

No time to see when woods we pass,
Where squirrels hide their nuts in grass:

No time to see in broad daylight,
Streams full of stars, like skies, at night…..

The man and woman observe that watching television is not France's favoured leisure activity. Although there is not much of a tourist infrastructure, the winter sun and cloudless skies draw local people from other, inland, villages. They come in their usual sophisticated sombre uniform of navy and black, and, as the neighbour says, pay attention to their proper walking boots. ('Attention, ne tombez pas, ')

Around the étang, there is a circular footpath, impressively managed, no potholes. Every few metres are notices with information and images of local flora/ fauna and especially,

seabirds(flamingos, cormorants, terns, herons,) and also, fish.

People carefully read the plaques, some taking photos, all in discussion.

The man thinks he has a personal resemblance to the grumpiest looking heron, (L'Héron cendré).

The woman, no ornithologist, will have to study this. Her knowledge of birds is mainly of the cuckoo, owl and blackbird type.

Now, in October, it's the eel season, fishing nets put out ready for the catch.

Today, there is a demonstration of the specialty of the Region- 'La Bourride'(eel stew). It's in the enormous meeting hall- the Palais de congrès.

The woman is interested in building on her cookery repertoire.

A trestle table is laid with eels, white fish, carrots, leeks, bouquet garni, garlic fennel, wine. A large cooking pot appears and a calor gas cooker, with timer. All to be masterminded today by the celebrity chef. The large group is looking forward to it.

The start is an unusually short lecture, about the history of the cuisine and region, a discussion about the ingredients and then - it's time to cook.

This is not to be a 'Ready steady cook !' experience. The celebrity chef has to get his matches. Walking away, 'Come back later, 'he calls, 'perhaps in 3 hours?'

In the spring there is a fair (not a funfair or clothes or jumble,) but an exhibition of local plants, viticulture, wild life. As if at a giant nature table, people enthusiastically sniff, taste and fill - out helpful questionnaires. The tables fill the huge hall. As usual, it is followed by a meal.

Definitely more sociable than watching television.

The Dropouts.

But improving the mind, or having a job, does not seem to be everybody's favourite, even though the French retire from work earlier than most.

The woman, walking the dog, regularly meets the same people everyday. They know the dog. Perhaps they are 'en route' to the Boulodrome, or heading for a bar to sit and chat to their friends. Calling in at the Tabac is an option.

Today is a slow, hot Sunday. The neighbour, a middle aged, good looking Frenchman- Claude-' un bel homme', is calling the woman. He has news. His father, who the woman knew, has died. He led a long life and lived to 90.

In his working life he had been a dentist. He hoped that Claude would show an interest. One day he took his son to show him the surgery. The boy found this so traumatic, not only did he decide never to be a dentist, but also never to work. He wants no part in this 'money obsessed 'society. No desire for le 'travail alimentaire'. (Working to put food on the table.) This is a one man personal protest against capitalism.

He is asked the question, what do you want to be when you grow up? Now at 55, he still hasn't decided.

He likes to chat to the man, who asks him about his plans. He doesn't have any. No need to turn on the tv, or open a newspaper. Speaking English, he says he is trying some painting, or maybe some music…. but it is 'doing his head in'.

If this is midlife retirement, it seems to suit him. To be too involved, to be too ambitious, is never good. He prefers to sit and watch the world go by, 'mise en scène' or rather like a theatre stage set after all he has the house his hardworking dentist father left him…

The Lake Isle of Innisfree, WB Yeats.

…And I shall have some peace there, for peace comes dropping slow

Dropping from the veils of the morning to where the cricket sings.

There midnight's all a glimmer and noon a purple glow,

And evening full of the linnet's wings..

I will arise and go now, for always night and day

I hear lake water lapping with low sounds by the shore:

While I stand on the roadway, or on the pavements gray,

I hear it in the deep heart's core.

Sitting outside, in a thick coat, in the boiling sun, is another neighbour. He drinks a fair bit of vin ordinaire and varies in coherence. He has a small vocabulary- 'Buongiorno'-or 'café?'- or 'Eengleesh!'. When he isn't sitting with his head in his hands thinking, he may walk a dog. It could be his. Or he may be busy, hanging up his shirts in his window to dry.

There is a gentlemanly, elderly Frenchman sitting carefully in the street. Coincidentally, he is by the cash machine.

He has a small canvas chair. It suits his small frame. He holds an oversized, old, mobile phone. There is a hat on the ground beside him and a handwritten notice. Roughly translated it says 'When you are too old and ugly to be 'escort boy', there is always the hat'……

The woman passes him most days when walking the dog. He is deferential, polite, softly spoken. 'Do you have somewhere to sleep?' she asks.

'Oh yes, Madame' replies, the man. 'I have a very comfortable flat in the city.'

But…. It is not all sunshine and red wine. There is the day to day business of living, and it's more difficult in French.

To start with the couple and their French counterparts seem to be polar opposites. Whilst they don't mind the French fondness for dressing all year in navy and black, (a kind of uniform which they find depressing,)they also seem to have quite different temperaments.

The man and woman seem to possess the legendary 'sang -

froid'. How can this be a French phrase? Not evident at the Post Office, the Tax Office, or often, the Health Centre. Is there anger here about something? Have they unknowingly walked in on an argument?

Perhaps it's their less than perfect French.

The man is told that the jobs are difficult. What all of them?

Perhaps…

No, it's 'Comme il faut', or doing what is necessary.

À la Poste, or the forgotten glasses.

Luckily for the woman, her neighbour, described as 'exuberant' is a post office counter clerk. This assistant comes under the 'fonctionnaire' category, rather like English civil servants, (no further similarity).

But, on this morning, she has a day off- blank stares when the woman asks if she might be in later?

Ploughing on, the woman boldly hands over her parcel to be processed. Quite straightforward-address clearly printed, senders' address on the back, as per protocol, she thought. No. There is another form to be filled out, in triplicate. Sadly, the woman has not brought her glasses. She can't read the small print.

She explains, apologetically, (of course). The counter clerk leans in, perhaps to offer help? thinks the woman.

Afraid not. 'Why haven't you brought your glasses?'

A challenging question to which there is no answer! Bravely, she asks if the assistant could kindly assist -and fill out the form?

With much huffing, puffing and eye- rolling, the assistant laboriously, completes the form. 'Is she always left-handed? Does she always write in that careful, curly writing?'

The woman's fixed smile keeps her from flinching. As she walks towards the door she leaves the smile behind. The queue stretches as far as the main exit.

The walk of shame.

She will ask the exuberant neighbour for her work schedule next time.

They understand there is a French way of getting round the many 'rules.' The woman is out with the dog and passes a house where there is a well-known, angry, territorial dog. As it is forbidden to put a warning notice on the door saying that- the notice on the door reads, 'le propriétaire du chien est méchant!'

The Angry Dog Owner

À la poste (part 2)

The woman has a parcel to return. Remembering the last time- she asks the man, 'Are you free?'

No. Right. Today, in November, it is not so hot, so she can carefully plan a strategy. First thought, is the exuberant neighbour working today?

It's 'bonne chance 'as there is the neighbour. She is dealing patiently and resignedly with Monsieur Gaillard.

He has a parcel too, but his is partly unwrapped. 'Why is your parcel open, Monsieur Gaillard?' With a small, quite kindly shrug, she accepts his answer' I wanted to look inside'. D'accord. Next question 'Why is the sender address on the back in somebody else's name?'

Ah yes, it's Monsieur Gaillard's daughter. Of course.

After the usual stamping of codes etc, Monsieur Gaillard happily heads for the door, but he is called back. This is the moment thinks the woman when he will be given The Lecture. She is wrong.

Monsieur Gaillard' the neighbour chirps, 'you have left your purse behind. '

Ah 'Merci, 'he says. He is smiling brightly. 'Bon après- midi et bonne journée!. '

Au Supermarché, or the Tarte aux myrtilles.

The best time to shop is before the car park turns into a hot oven. Nobody about. The woman, being speedy, expects a quick whizz around the shelves. No time for sociability. Long chats are out, just a 'bonjour' or two, and home. In no time she is heading for the checkout, all going to plan. She carefully avoids the customer trying to queue jump, holding up one item, but with a large basket of goods to be checked out by her feet. The checkout boy is, as usual, polite, quick -and especially -non-chatty, but oh dear, no bar code on the tarte aux myrtilles. He tries the very long code on the packet, no good, and a second time... the supervisor summoned, the woman waits and waits The supervisor can't crack the code either. The woman decides that tarte aux myrtilles was never her favourite-'don't bother, ' she says. Not so easy, the bill has to be adjusted without the tart, another careful job. 'Why don't you want it? 'says the supervisor. 'Too much waiting. ' There are shrugs all round. The queue, patiently long and used to long codes, watches her as she heads for the car park.

She sees a neighbour who explains, 'but this is the south Madame. '

The man says he prefers tarte tartin (apple tart) anyway.

And......the dog biscuit saga or the red jacketed assistant.

The dog is a small dog, but a big eater. The woman buys special' light biscuits' -only available from one supermarket. 'I'll pop over at lunch time,' she says, 'everyone will be busy, It will be quiet.' She' s right - just a handful of cars in the huge car park, but why is that handful queued at the 'fast' checkout?

Where are the smart red jacketed assistants?

She takes her light biscuits to the self service checkout. It can't be that difficult- and good, there is a red jacketed assistant nearby, cleaning the tills. Bag placed in the bagging area, tick for the credit card, does she want a ticket says the machine? No, she won't bother.

But, what's this - the exit barrier, firmly closed. The red jacketed lady is still busily cleaning, head down.

Another customer manages to move the barrier and help. The woman gets out. Things seem ok, but as she leaves, the red jacketed assistant is running after her shouting loudly, accusingly and embarrassingly. 'Votre carte de credit ne marche pas' (doesn't work). How stern she looks. A face like thunder. The Woman goes back, does the whole procedure again, the assistant ignores her efforts. The barrier stays down again. Now what?

Another kindly customer leans over and carefully explains 'you need to scan your QR code to get out'…

'Comme il faut'- of course.

The red jacketed assistant doesn't look up.

The dog make-over

Dog Days

The Dog Days of summer may have their origin in Greek history and are nothing to do with dogs, but on the Mediterranean coast they are the scorching, sultry days of July and August, hot-even for the dog.

Everyone searches for shade. The olive and pine trees in the garden, now grown tall and leafy are shady canopies. The woman thinks about a hammock.

But back to the dog, still needing exercise. The woman seems to be in charge here- as the neighbour says, 'who holds the lead?'

The woman is puzzled by village dogs and their owners. Yes,

there is the pampered pooch in sparkling colour and top knot, usually with a striking resemblance to the owner- and always - very small.

This duo can be seen shopping at the dog boutique. Then there is the oversized dog, panting on a short tether being called back 'Viens ici'(Come here) What else. No wonder they bare their teeth. Then there are the hunting dogs, lean, hungry, slinky-and silent, no leads, no collars and mainly let out of a car boot to run wild.

Codes of behaviour are taken seriously: not clearing dog mess, punishable by a large fine, is upheld by municipal police or wardens; No need for scrawled private notices, or threatening messages about video cameras. The village has invested in prohibitive measures, bins, bags. And then there's the man on the motorbike suction machine: we all politely wish him 'Bonjour!' and 'Bonne Journée!'. Caught out (without a bag) one morning-a lady in a nightdress, is calling, 'Where is the machine?'

The Dog and the Vet.

This is a different environment for the dog-she has yearly vaccinations, very comprehensive, covering all the known Mediterranean canine diseases, or so they are told.

They set off at a fast trot, what a lovely day for a walk!

At the surgery door, the dog senses danger and tries to make a run for it.

Never mind dog, it will soon be over.

They present their papers: vaccination records, medical history, is the passport needed? What about weight?

'Stand on the scales….. hmm. 'Ok at the moment, but don't let her get any fatter.'

The injection is done in a flash-they dash to the door.. 'Joyeux Noel!' says the Vet. 'Bonne Année' they reply, even though it's only August.

A veterinary emergency, (or there is only one solution to every problem.)

One afternoon the dog wakes up from a siesta in distress, rushing from room to room, shaking her head in a crazy way. The man and woman try techniques for calming; rubbing ears, attempts at instilling ear solution etc. This doesn't work. No hesitation, just call our acquaintance of 20 years, the Vet, he will help. The answering machine says 'open later. ' She leaves a message, please ring her back with advice or an appointment.

The woman tries again to calm the dog. 'Take the phone to the top floor', says the man, 'so that you can speak to the Vet when he rings.'

He doesn't ring.

Luckily, the dog eventually calms down.

The next day the woman goes to the Cabinet. ' I had a problem yesterday' she says. 'Yes, we heard your message. We were not doing emergencies only planned appointments and you didn't have an appointment.'

The woman thinks about searching for another Vet.

No jewelled harness today

The dog, like everyone else, needs smartening up.

The woman goes to the village boutique for a new dog bowl. She is not persuaded to buy a jewelled harness.

For any dog living here, it can be very hot. Especially with a thick bushy coat. From time to time an appointment is made with the 'toilettage' van. This is a lengthy appointment in a van, set up like a medical cabinet-a professionally uniformed lady, scissors and watch in top pocket, calm and smiling. The dog likes her, trots happily up the steps, tail wagging and- it all starts with the jar of treats.

This is a sort of mobile Vet, qualifications papering the interior. There is grooming, trimming, shampooing. in fact, the dog is treated like … a dog. There is no howling, no barking and the dog looks, and smells, much better.

Authority or Authoritarianism? or 'just do what they say.'

Today, the woman is able to test out the theory that the 'French police take themselves very seriously' and 'you don't discuss things with the police, just do what they say'.

As she attempts to drive across the road, to filter into the filling station, she observes a large blue car with flashing lights and a siren going. 'Les Gendarmes'. There must be a problem somewhere she thinks. Wrong. it seems she is the problem. She pulls up on the forecourt of the garage. A face at the car window, definitely not feeling the need to be friendly, leans in. 'Can I help you officer?' she says. 'Car keys,' is the answer. No pleasant preamble here. She hands over her car keys. 'Driving licence, insurance documents, Log book. '

'What is the problem please?' she asks. No answer.

'Get back'- pointing to the ground. The woman's 'pardon?' is greeted with ' Parlez Français'. Maximum intimidation.

Two policeman, (armed as usual) walk around her car, kicking the tyres and taking photographs -she assumes of the number plate. She is not the intimidated sort, after all, nobody is born submissive. She begins to feel angry.

The woman is amazed at the rudeness of the officer, and asks him why he is speaking like this. It doesn't seem to be a good thing to say, obviously he is not used to being challenged. She explains that, actually, she is now blocking the forecourt exit and points to the roundabout, explaining in English, that she will drive around that- and then speak to him. He shakes his head(understanding her English this time apparently.)He blocks the bonnet of her car.

The female officer asks, 'do you know why we pulled you over?' The woman, - 'perhaps I'm blocking the Launderette entrance.' No, it appears she has filtered across a solid white line. Ah. 'sorry'. The woman apologises. The female officer, with a very faint flicker of a smile says, 'if you're asked by the police to stop, that is what you do. Immediately. We won't fine you today- but take this as a warning.'

Shakily, the woman totters into the filling station, where there seems to be a group of grinning people. 'Bad luck' they say. It is obviously the best thing they've seen all day.

'A solid white line was painted there yesterday.'

The woman reflects on this at home: yes, the police do take themselves very seriously indeed.

She wonders if the gendarme has read the checkout reminder for the staff of a local supermarket. It reads 'Le respect ne coûte rien mais ça rapporte beaucoup' (respect costs nothing, but the pay off is much).

In this post revolutionary Republic, it is difficult to see Where fraternité, égalité, Liberté fits.

What of my human rights when talking to the policemen? she wonders. Does liberté mean that you can speak up for yourself? (even the school girl next door can talk about her 'rights.) She discusses this with her neighbour, 'just give them what they want. '

The woman sympathises with the neighbours, who try to teach her how to get round the rules. The difference is that this is all they know.

In order to live sanely in France as a resident, rather than a holiday maker, the woman reasons that everyone needs to understand three things: the environment and most aspects of life here are influenced by government funds, devolved locally. With this funding comes rules, and their interpretation varies.

For example, the roads have impeccable tarmac, a village square litter free, despite street markets happening three times a week. Litter collectors are out before the last stall is packed away. Free dog bag dispensers and bins stand at street corners, flower beds are replanted with every season, Palm trees and pines are lopped. Any 'best kept' award would surely be won by this village and police patrol every day.

Everyone respects this environment.

They say if the cemetery is well cared for the Mayor is 'au courant'. So far, so good.

This should be an idyllic, trouble -free environment. But, it comes with a downside of 'rules, regulations, and 'interdit' notices. Everybody comments that this is a bureaucratic nightmare. The couple are unused to being told how to live…sometimes even by other' citizens. They wonder why people are assumed to be naive, naughty children. Beware the wagging finger and the 'Non!'

There are extra arrows telling you which way to go down a one way street (where there are already arrows), other pedestrians will tell you which side to walk on a footpath, cyclists will pummel straight at you because you are on a cycle track and they have right of way, shop assistants will peer into your shopping bag, security guards will guard shop exits.

Whether people feel irritated or protected is hard to say. it's unlikely that there can ever be only one solution to every problem. But it does remove any decision making from anyone 'in charge', or from anyone else.

It has been said that people hate bureaucracy but can't live without it.

The couple, like everyone else have to employ ex-fonctionnaires to help them interpret the rules. Often it's just' grit through 'the unpleasantness.

And, there seems to be a big difference between authority and authoritarianism. Maybe it's easy to get it wrong.

The Municipal policeman, are often kindly, sometimes neutral, but never aggressive. They can be very helpful: this week was one of those Mediterranean stormy days. It started with a whirling wind, eerily the street lights came on, flickered and went out. The underground cisterns' pump lights lit up and the warning siren sounded. The neighbour was out looking at his stick in the lake. (It's his private flood warning).

What to do? There was a knock on the door, two Municipal policeman. 'As there is a storm coming, we suggest you move your car to higher ground- and close your shutters. Perhaps move upstairs and sit it out, you need blocks to put under your furniture?'

> *The Police Municipale, or local police are employed directly by the Mairie. Unlike the gendarmerie they have no military background, their job is to maintain a safe environment.*
> *They can be seen outside the school gates, taking fees from the market traders, or managing traffic.*
> *They usually know the local residents by name.*

Bonne Santé or... Good Health.

The reluctant dentist. (Part one.)

Daily life has its share of health checks; eyes, teeth etc.

The man chips a front tooth on an olive stone. How lucky it is that the dentist is just around the corner, a two minute walk away-and that it's the middle of a working week. 'See you shortly,' he calls to the woman, 'back for a cup of tea'. The man strolls over.... the cabinet appears to be locked. Perhaps there's a note? He's probably on holiday. Gone surfing perhaps? No note.

The tooth is uncomfortable and jagged. The man goes to the Mairie to take advice. 'Has the dentist retired, perhaps?' 'Possibly,' says the serious advisor/adjoint. 'Or maybe he's 'trying to retire. I know he's a keen surfer.'

……Aah.

La Maison de Santé.

When the man and woman first lived in the village, there was a village doctor. His tiny surgery (Le cabinet) was squeezed between the church, bells chiming every quarter of an hour, and the dog accessory boutique.

There was a tiny plaque on the wall with the doctor's name and qualifications.

On hot afternoons, he could be seen with his bag walking around the village, doing home visits. He worked on his own, answered his own phone, and, with occasional help from his wife, booked his own appointments. He was known to be a considerate man.

A consultation, despite appearing casual, was a serious affair. The conversations were formal, no familiarity, but a polite acknowledgement. The woman's, 'How are you?' was carefully ignored. No familiar' Tu'here. The French neighbour said that familiarity is considered unprofessional.

There was often a referral to a 'spécialiste ' arranged by the patient, (limited diagnostic equipment in the cabinet).

The 'Cardiologue' was popular.

Usually though, the local people were treated by this doctor, his office light illuminating the little square until late.

His son took over. The small surgery became a retro-photography shop and a new avant-garde, maison de santé opened, shaped like a wave, by the beach.

A wise friend says 'choose an old lawyer and a young doctor. '

All these doctors are young.

This group are even more formal, now technical people; maybe they recognise you maybe not. The woman is seen here by a doctor, fixing her with a steely stare behind steely spectacles, the black sweater completes the air of seriousness. He is known to be smart, but volatile. The couple are told by their neighbour that the definition of a good doctor, apart from being young, is to 'tell you what is the matter with you and tell you what pills to take'…exactly right. Sensitivity training not obvious. No question of ending the consultation with a pleasantry, no cheerful 'Bonne Journée' here.

Telling you what pills to take….

From the patient's point of view, there is a symbiosis between the pharmacy and the maison de santé, patients often preferring to speak to a sympathetic pharmacist(and it's free). The pharmacies and para -pharmacies are old, reliable institutions, dispensing health advice, but quick to say that they are not doctors. Their knowledge is encyclopaedic. In this village, there are five or six counter staff- all busy, no discrimination between pharmacist and préparatrice. Anyone can sell shampoo or equally advise on heart pills. There is no narrow attitude to medicine either, they may refer you to their stock of herbal or homeopathic products. Or they might help with enquiries about sophrology, healers, hynotherapy or reflexology. Perhaps 'sevrage tabagique' (stop smoking). Apparently, fatigue is a major problem for all ages, plus nervosité, insomnia and 'heavy legs'.

A new feature is the computerised astrology screen in the pharmacy window. Maybe that will give people what they want to hear.

The Spécialiste.

In France everyone has a heart check five yearly. This is always to be with the 'Spécialiste'.

This year, it's the man's turn. He knows the hospital and rings to fix a date.

As usual, the Cardiologue (heart specialist) only appears to work in the days of boiling heat- having an exercise test on an exercise bike is not very appealing, but the man makes his appointment.

The day before, the woman is driving through the city. 'I think I 'll just check the hospital parking arrangements. '

She heads down the hospital road. Where is the hospital?

On her left is a disused, overgrown with weeds, sort of building: under the greenery she can just make out a rusty 'Polyclinique' sign. The car park is now dug up.

Is there a redirection sign to another hospital? No.

She drives back, asks the neighbour. ' Oh yes, there's a new hospital now, ten kilometres away. '

Perhaps somebody could have mentioned it.

The man decides to leave the check - up for another five years.

Papers, Papers……

The woman is just leaving with the dog for their early promenade, when there is a crash and thump from the road outside. She leaves the dog and rushes out. Lying stretched out in the middle of the road is the neighbour's quite portly daughter, Beatrice. En route to have coffee with her mother opposite, she seems to have caught her foot in an uncovered drain and is calling intermittently

'Aidez-moi, 'and 'Pompiers!' Followed by,

'Papers, where are my Papers?'

The woman hopes somebody has the 'Papers'.

The man has arrived to see what the racket is about-

'Call the Pompiers, 'says Beatrice 'my shoulder is dislocated!'

'Can you feel your fingers Beatrice?' says the helpful man. Now the performance is in full swing. The woman is sitting in the road reassuring Beatrice, the elderly man at the end of the street positions himself to stop the traffic, the elderly wife is worried about where the Pompiers are.

'They might be miles away' she says.

The woman hopes Beatrice can't hear that. The sun is directly overhead and it is hot.

'Fetch a parasol!'

'What about Beatrice's mother?'

The mother is helped out into the street- what a shock - luckily she has taken 'un petit calmant'.

With much noise from sirens the Pompiers arrive. 'Ah, it's my cousin' says the mother.

'I remember you in short trousers.' Béatrice.

The mother is now sitting nearby on a comfortable chair(out of the sun). Impressively, the Pompiers get working. Blood pressure, oxygen, questions asked. Expertly a canvas is somehow slipped under Beatrice and in a trice she is lifted and heading for the ambulance. Everything going well.... except - something is bothering Beatrice.

'My Papers, where are my Papers?'

Ah……the relief for all -the elderly man is holding the handbag and, it contains -the Papers! Everybody waves as the ambulance pulls away.

(Authors note. In France it is obligatory to carry certain documents (papers) and cards to access health care.

The dentist (Part two)

Sometimes ' Comme il Faut' seems to be carried too far..

The neighbour has a new job. She is working as a dental receptionist at a new practice. The man is still searching for someone to repair his tooth.

'Fine', she says, 'I will phone you tomorrow and you can be seen as soon as a dentist is free.'

In the meantime she sends an email.

'Please send me three images of your broken tooth. Is it upper or lower jaw, front or back, what type of tooth is it?'

'I will need to discuss this with the dentist before you arrive' she writes.

The man arrives promptly but without the images, the next day, the dentist manages to patch it up.

Now for the Papers(naturally in triplicate). Here is a 3 page dossier, called a 'devis' or estimate, detailing various tooth replacements and treatments.

'I'll have the best, 'says the man.

Good: there is only one drawback, the new surgery is now closed for a 4 week renovation.

Meanwhile, the woman is walking the dog; there seems to be a light glowing behind the village dentist's shutters. She tries the door, he is back.

The surfing season must be over.

Quickly the man nips over, makes a rendez-vous and within 2 weeks he has a new front tooth(no forms, no codes, no images, no Papers).

'It can be done you see' says the man.'

'Acquainted with the night' Robert Frost or 'L'heure Bleue.

I have been one acquainted with the night.
I have walked out in rain-and back in rain.
I have outwalked the furthest city light.

I have looked down the saddest city lane.
I have passed by the watchman on his beat
And dropped my eyes, unwilling to explain.

I have stood still and stopped the sound of feet
When far away an interrupted cry
Came over houses from another street.
But not to call me back or say goodbye;
And further still at an unearthly height,
One luminary clock against the sky
Proclaimed the time was neither wrong nor right,
I have been one acquainted with the night.

City of Light

Many French people will say they have lived in Paris. Apparently only in Paris do people not complain of boredom, but conversely, many French people say they can't stand the Parisians. They are 'snob', says the neighbour.

They ask us, 'is it very sunny where you live?' It is. (in the south even two-year-olds wear sunglasses.)

And, 'do you jouez à la pétanque(play boules) all day?' Yes.

The woman, like everyone else, has her own images of this northern city, this is mainland Europe. When she tells her neighbour Celine about her writing, the reply is 'You must start with Paris.' (French people are proud of being French.)

So the couple revisit Paris.

Staying in the most bohemian part of the city, they hope it will still be vibrantly alternative: things don't necessarily get better.

Outside their hotel, young crowds turn the streets into an international University. They squeeze past outstretched legs, straddling the pavements. No attempt to move out of the way here.

To start with they have to deal with the weather.

It is bitterly cold and snowing. A white blanket deadens the traffic. The pavements are rinky icy. People disguised in balaclavas slide past, clinging to walls. The street cleaners have left a legacy of water, now frozen.

Finding a café and huddling by an outdoor heater, they seem to have joined the morning office workers having a debrief.

Of course, the city looks beautiful, it's surprising that the colour red is so appealing.

The woman remembers that this city is walkable -and she has her street map. The grand Haussmann boulevards are tricky, five lanes of careering traffic in the snow, mixed with the shrill whistles of the gendarmes. E - scooters and Vélib bikes sliding by on the pavements and boulevards.

But she has a plan, maybe a museum/gallery, and then a gastronomic feast.

The man has a different plan, he would like to get his bearings with a birds eye view of the city. He aims for the observation deck of the tallest building in 'Paris Proper'-the Montparnasse tower. Let's hope the rooftop is not closed today…

Climbing White Stork Tower. Tang variations.

If you want to see a thousand miles then go up another floor, always up.

The woman leaves him to enjoy the 60 floors. She will not repeat the previous Tour Eiffel dining experience. Too high.

The youngest son is calling over today from London for a business meeting. The woman plans to meet him in a quiet space, preferably green.

'Try Le Jardin du Luxembourg.'

It is exactly as calm as she expects.

Children are still well wrapped up, sailing model boats, watching a puppet show or waving from a vintage carousel.

The youngest son is already sitting in a gazebo and asks 'What kept you?'

Exploring the city, there is magic in the air. The woman wonders if she has an overactive imagination.. Is she hallucinating when she sees the ghost of Ernest Hemingway shooting pigeons in the Luxembourg gardens, or maybe Renoir painting the Bal de Moulin de Galette. Is that Picasso, in a marinière of course, in his studio in the Bateau -lavoir?'

She is looking forward to lunch alone later, in a hilltop restaurant, with great views. She wants to disprove what she has been told- that Parisian waiters are rude.

'Madame will wait for Monsieur?' asks the waiter. She explains' toute seule Monsieur.'

(Monsieur is not joining me).

She waits and waits …

Eventually, the waiter returns. By now she has had a lengthy time to study the menu, so orders confidently.

'Un hors -d'œuvre de gésiers' followed by 'poisson du jour, s'il vous plaît. '

'Vous avez mal choisi, Madame' says the waiter. What a disgrace.

Perhaps she will do better at the Art Deco cinema. She knows that this is a gem of a place, small armchairs to sit in, wall-to-wall screen and very warm.

The film is eccentric, thoughtful and moving. She loves it.

Afterwards, she glides and slides down the street with the theme tune in her ears:

'On the Champs-Élysées, on the Champs-Élysées! In the Sun, in the rain at noon at midnight Everything you could want is on

The Champs-Élysées. !'

Now it's getting late, twilight, or more romantically, ' L'heure Bleue.'

Just easing into the evening, in a bar with zinc top tables, she can sit here and pretend to be pensively French.

A book selection from the window bookshelf, a glass of wine(not absinthe) and it's a good day after all.

The next day the snow is temporarily easing and it's one of insistent Paris rain, interspersed with biblical downpours. Passing Renoir's house, it's no wonder he painted 'Les Parapluies'. (umbrellas).

Better buy an umbrella-plenty to choose from.

'You can't leave Paris, without visiting one of the famous cimitières,' (cemeteries) says the Concierge.

This is to be another history lesson. Politicians, philosophers artists, actors, writers are all to be found here.

Today, the man is wearing his city clothes, ankle length black coat and beret. Searching for the grave of Serge Gainsbourg, he notices a small, silent group standing near a freshly dug plot. About to hurry away in respectful silence, he is called back(Oh no, now what?)

'Are you the Curé?'

Next time, try wearing smart, casual.

On their last night the man tells the concierge he hasn't been as cold or wet as this since Moscow.

In the darkening winter light, the woman heads to the Abbey. This seems appropriate to her mood.

She finds a side door and slips into the Nun's Priory. A calming sanctuary. The look and feel of an exercise yard, without room to actually exercise. Compline, the final office of the day, will soon begin. A screen slides aside, a group of nuns noiselessly arrive. The Gregorian chant, waves of notes rising and falling, the soprano voices are beautiful and uplifting.

There is no music, no hymn numbers and no other voices.

The traffic rattles on, but nobody can hear it.

Today, it's Christmas Day in the south, the narrow village streets empty and silent. A solitary dog taking itself for a Christmas walk. Unusually, everyone is indoors feasting, normally meal times happen elsewhere. People are closed in behind warm doors. Looking around, it is unclear as to the meaning of this feast. Perhaps it's a midwinter family get -together, maybe something holy -or is it a giant toy town event, intended for children?

If there is any kind of debate of God versus santa, today, santa seems to be in the lead.

Joyeux Noel

Models of santa claus climb the walls of most houses, giant models of toy soldiers are stationed outside the Mairie, a special wooden letterbox is dedicated to letters to santa, toy bears are hidden in the palm trees. Does santa still visit every home in one night? No nativity scenes in sight, and yet walking past the Catholic church, it is packed, extra chairs out, people standing in the doorway.

Toy town

She reflects that in this traditional community, the church is still seen as a comforting certainty.

Now it's mid -January, it is freezing Mediterranean winter. The wind blows from the Pyrenees and howls through the village. The couple, used to warm wet westerly winds, find cold and clear very different. Not surprisingly, all that's left of the market is one chicken van, with two brave customers. The woman, feeling frozen, decides not to walk the dog... and the neighbour suggests she buys her a warm dog jacket (the boutique.)

Looking for a sheltered side street, she hears the sound of excited conversation. Probably two dozen, healthy looking, mainly women, come around the corner, enthusiastically waving walking poles. They walk in unison. Of course, this is the walking group. The woman, politely says 'bonjour' about twenty times. By now, she's warmed up. It seems there's a celebration. It's the New Year's walk.

The leader tells the woman that they have all walked for four hours (in the icy wind) and are looking forward to a postponed, warm, New Year's Day lunch. 'Bon appétit.'

Today, the woman is a 'femme de ménage'(housewife.) After all, the usual washing, cleaning, ironing, shopping, goes on, wherever you live.

In the long, hot days of summer, washing dries in a morning, but it is midwinter, the sun is weak-so she goes to La Laverie Automatique, (launderette).

The neighbour, a smiling kind looking man on a bench in the winter sun, waves her off.

The launderette is a complicated place apparently, judging by the number of official notices and instructions on the various walls and on the machines. She searches for her money. Aah, the machines don't take credit cards, coins, or apparently notes, so what do they take? They take tokens obtainable from the nearby garage. Right.

She manoeuvres the dials on the dryer. Does she want hot, very hot or lukewarm? What a choice. Thankfully, the machine works, but she is interrupted by an agitated customer. 'Is this your washing? 'He points at the dryer.

It seems all the other machines are busy. He will have to wait- hold on a minute -but he's in a hurry…. 'tant pis' (too bad) she thinks.

The woman collects up her bone -dry, washing, 'Passez une bonne journée, Monsieur, 'she says sweetly.

On her return, the neighbour is still sitting on the bench, gently nodding.

Le Cabinet d'infirmière.

It's still January but now the wind has turned from a freezing blast, to a gentle breeze. The woman calls this a 'cat's paw wind.'

'Winter is over, ' says the neighbour.

Without wearing her usual winter bundle of clothes, the woman walks around the corner to the nurses' cabinet for an annual check. This is a no appointment drop- in centre, a stand alone surgery run by registered nurses.

There is a group of chatty clients/ patients sitting about in an open plan room. They look mainly able -bodied and rosy cheeked. The quite tatty health posters on the walls don't seem to be of interest.

One nurse is efficiently dealing with everything. A sort of village Accident and Emergency centre, without the fear. Anyone with bandages and walking sticks is soon dispatched and on their way, blood tests are completed, money is collected.

The woman reflects on why it's so relaxed here, no ringing phones, no secretaries who could be called officious. No terrified patients or remote doctors.

Gentle music plays in the background.

The people, having been dealt with, seem reluctant to leave. The woman likes the camaraderie. ' I am glad to be alive' says one octogenarian, 'but the doctors still can't cure old age.'

The woman joins in, confidently thinking she is on good form. Her French, surely, is coming on well. She wonders if her efforts to speak French makes her sound like somebody else. The nurse turns to her. 'You have a very pretty accent she says. The woman beams. The nurse adds, 'very Anglais.'

The Post Office girl.

It is surprising that people who work in the more ordinary jobs, and on their own -seem to be much happier -perhaps they work to their own timetable, they are freer.

They seem to work very hard.

Most of the deliveries in the village use electric bikes or electric vans, silently manoeuvering the narrow streets. The Post Office girl has a yellow electric bike which she rides happily, sometimes on the wrong side of the road and even into icy wind. Today, she's not so happy. The woman has a regular delivery of a global newspaper. As it's written in English It keeps her up-to-date with world news and is published once a week. The problem is that it is only sporadically delivered. The woman goes to the post office and asks where it is. Her enquiry is treated very seriously, the story is ramped up. Her address is written down, phone number taken, and a small synopsis of the problem. Half an hour later, there is a crashing banging at the door. It is Post Office girl. 'I understand your newspaper has not been delivered.. I would like to explain that this is not my fault. The paper has not been delivered to us.' 'Oh I see,' says the woman, 'obviously not the problem.'

The next morning, there is another loud bang on the door. Here is Post Office girl, beaming. She hands over the paper, 'it's come now !' The woman offers effusive thanks. Post Office girl is a hero.

Heritage or 'Le Patrimoine.'

The woman notices a new looking black wheelchair advancing down the street. It is the neighbour who never goes out, being pushed by her strong daughter. Dressed for a special trip, they are excitedly smiling.

The woman is pleased to see them. The elderly neighbour has come out to read the notice boards with their black and white photography, recently put up around the streets. They explain the village history.

'Did you know that nobody knows the origin of the name 'Rue Paradis?' Of course, it is the escape route from pirate invasion.

The neighbour is relaxed and happy, she has seen a photo of her mother on the outdoor washing place (L'Ancien Lavoir) and is proud that her family go back many generations.

Family

Meanwhile their 'courtyard garden' as an Englishman disappointedly called it, is doing well. The olive tree has matured, and the vine and the bay. The cypress is surviving.

The woman is proudly watching the progress of her orange pip, taking from a fresh orange. It will definitely be a sturdy plant she hopes, if small.

The umbrella pine has been riskily pruned by the man- as the volunteered expert came once - and never returned. The neighbour says he is known to be a ' Bonjour, Au Revoir man'(hello, goodbye).

The only let-down in this idyllic space is the concrete garden wall, grey, distressed and ugly.

Who can help here?

The lady opposite will know, she is bound to be in-as she very rarely goes out. Yes, she knows just the person, a self-employed painter and his workman (ouvrier). He charges a bit, but he is meticulous, ('perfectionist', she says). Maybe.

A very smart Frenchman arrives on a classy motorbike. He carries a leather file and is wearing a mariniére top (only the beret is missing). He draws up measurements, inspects the garden and surround from all angles, and discusses what he will, and particularly what he will not, do. He tells them he is free in 4 to 5 months. Working on Midi time, they are not in a hurry.

After the heat of summer, the Master Painter arrives. His workman will be joining him later, after he has helped with the baby. There is a swift change into working gear, still much smarter than most.

He gets to work immediately …at 7. 30 in the morning. The woman offers coffee. No thank you.

The Master Painter works solidly preparing the courtyard/garden wall. On the dot at mid-day, he leaves.

The next morning (at7. 30am) the garden gate creaks open. Two workers this time. 'How is the baby now ? 'the woman asks the ouvrier as he gets out the scaffolding.

'What baby?' he says.

With or without a baby, the ouvrier and Master Painter work without stopping. The scaffolding is up, and ready.

The plan is to use a type of coloured plaster for the walls, this will be sprayed on by machine and smoothed by hand. It is called l'enduit. The couple are left to decide on a colour. The woman likes vieille rose, a faded pink. ' Do you think we have to ask the Mairie if it's suitable?'

The next day, the Master Painter mixes the colour. It looks frighteningly pink. 'Like it?' he says. Oh dear, we don't dare ask him to mix it all again.

Miraculously, the next morning the colour has dried. It is now a soft, glowing rose.

Now, several years on, it is still glowing. A credit to the Master Painter and his workman. The woman sends a photo to an English friend in England. 'I love it, she says, I have walked down my street and there isn't a pink house, or pink garden wall in sight.

The couple are told that it is unusual to find a non- complaining Frenchman. They test this out in the village Tabac.

This small shop seems to be a hub of cheerfulness. Even the lighted cigar sign outside looks optimistic in a dark street. Somewhere to go to pass an hour or two. The surprisingly portly Patron dispenses not only cigarettes and lottery tickets, but also wisdom and bonhomie. Nobody seems to be buying his stock of ladies scarves,

wine, children's toys, penknives. Instead he gives his full attention to handfuls of lottery tickets, patiently checking numbers and then, handing back handfuls of euro notes.

Le Patron tells the woman proudly that he is multilingual and particularly good at English and German. He hasn't noticed yet that the woman is English. She tries out an English sentence. A puzzled silence. Luckily he is rescued: other customers arrive and unfazed, he switches smoothly into French.

(Next time, when the shop is empty, she thanks him for trying).

No complaining going on here.

They say that's it's no longer revolutionary to be bored by politics and religion. The young say routine is boring. The couple, older, never really were 'cool or boring' anyway. For them, quality of life is the new slogan.

For many of the retired, the boulodrome offers just the right mix of sociability, competition and skill. If you meet a friend on a weekday he is carrying his personal boules set and saying ' Je boule.' There is a special uniform for this, (red) and prizes. The friend has won an oil painting.

On non -match days, he can be seen playing solitarily…on his own…

In this village, dominated by wind and water, it is not only the sea birds who ' catch the wind.' But there is always a fine balance between too little and too much. The sailors, sand yachtsmen, surfers and kite surfers, all study the wind variations. Some people have diplomas in every kind of wind sport.

> *The man being a sailor, has become an expert on Mediterranean winds. The neighbour tells him that the usual wind, the 'Tramontane' is a dry northerly wind from the mountains.*
> *The ' Marin' less popular, blows from the south but brings sea fret, haze and -smells of salt.*
> *The Sirocco from the Sahara is hot and dry and can set temperatures on 'broil'.*

Today, a small crowd is gathering on the beach. Something is going on. A home -made wind sock has appeared. A man is lying on the sand. Perhaps there has been an accident.

Not the case. Amid a tangle of leather and motors and parachutes, someone is strapping themselves into a complicated harness, fixing what looks like a lawn mower engine to their back. This, the woman is told, is powered paragliding. A respectful silence follows while the man performs safety checks, talks on a mobile, perhaps checking wind speed?

He starts to run along the beach, pity there are no cliffs to jump off, thinks the woman. He finds a slope, jumps, but lands in a tangle on the sand. The crowd resist any urge to rescue him. They stand back. Here he is running again, hold your breath, another 'Aaaah…'as he hits the sand again. Better not give up yet.

One more go, hooray, lift off. Collective cheering. From his armchair in the sky, the man waves.

Some people prefer a more gentle approach, no noisy lawn-mower motor-just powered by wind and water, floating in air, like the sea birds.

The Kite Surfer

No wonder all this is called 'extreme sports' says the man. For him, not being one of life's joiners, the appreciation of nature soothes his mind. Being a country boy, a walk in the woods is just as good as risking your life in the sky. A walk around the lake, a seat just watching the seabirds, not competing with them; or sitting companionably and silently with a neighbour(language skills not required).

'You are what you wear.'

Today, the woman is meeting her impeccably coiffed friend Mireille, for coffee(known as 'une pause -café'- but lasts longer). This is in the main village square, 'la place'.

Nobody here has heard the expression 'grabbing a coffee.' This is a leisurely chat, some local news, some family updates, some politics, but mainly it's about friendship.

Mostly too, it's people watching.

Mireille has been once to England. She understands that there is a complicated social class system there. ' How do you work out who is who 'she asks. 'Is it by the way they dress?'. 'No', says the woman, ' it's by the way they speak. '

This is news to Mireille, looking at her, and almost everyone else, there seems to be an innate sense of style; of presentation. Elegance is an attitude they say. No fashion victims here. The woman wonders why black, navy and white are made for each other. (She thinks longingly of red and green, switch it up a bit).

'And colour?' She asks.

'Fine for children', says Mireille.

Mireille tell a story. She has been to a 'girls only' hotel break. They share rooms. The hotel has a shoe cleaning service.

'Leave your shoes outside the door Mireille. They are Cartier.'

At first the woman has the immigrant mindset of 'wanting to fit in.' Her friend never appears without earrings, matching necklace and -something tastefully black.

She is up for the challenge. Mireille advises classical, elegant and especially- stylish.

On a day when the woman is looking particularly 'unstylish' and is in the street in gardening shoes, she now knows that the stares she is getting are not of admiration. She takes note of what other people are wearing and tries to copy them. With no plans to be a fashionista, to be 'chic 'here seems to be only a matter of wearing three items, the jeans(blue), the dress(black) the trench (beige) the marinière, (blue and white stripes), to cheer it up. A kind of universal blue - on - black.

The woman and her friend go shopping. She is steered away from the chain stores with their rails of appealing cheerful bright colours(vulgar), fashion items and glamour. Mireille, who is wise, says 'baggy clothes never look as good as they feel.'

Here, the fit is more important than the garment.

In the absence of the little dressmakers of the past, they instead go to a small boutique in a side street. Greeted at the door by Madame, Mireille explains that they need style advice. Madame regards the woman carefully, then directs her to the 'Cabines Essayage' (changing rooms).

She is handed a careful selection of clothes to try on. 'Let's get this over.' She thinks.

The woman does as she is told: emerging to ….. silence. I don't really think navy, black and beige are my colours, do you?

French chic.

Desiderata -Ehrmann

Go placidly amid the noise and the haste, and remember what peace there may be in silence….

The thing about walking a cocker spaniel is that the dog is bred to track- this means that it never walks in a straight line. The woman tries to avoid having the lead wrapped around her ankles and landing- as the man says 'On the deck'(face down)

Today, in winter, they are on the beach, a shore walk, almost the only people there. Perhaps the occasional beachcomber or' man in a van.' Sometimes there are hippie types hanging out their washing, or maybe a lone camper van with a person on the step- in fluffy slippers and wearing rubber gloves.

It is a beautiful silent winter day. There are three tiny boats on the horizon- motionless. The sea has changed from summer deep blue to winter shiny silver.

It's difficult to imagine the 'Mosquito' Bar, the swimmers, the rows of parasols -of a few months ago. The woman sits on a rock and just looks...

A *Different Place.*

The woman is going to the local city.. It has a Cathedral and academic buildings -so she calls it a city. This is a different place. Whereas village life has been about community and 'quartier' this is anonymous. It is modern, avant-garde even, impatient and quick. Scooters fly past on the pavements, traffic hurls around the roundabouts. The air fizzes with energy.

But surprisingly, all is calm on the boulevards. To sit, happily 'toute seule' with a small black coffee is to watch the world go by. On this day in winter, she can now turn towards the sun. Later, she reflects on the changes in 25 years- the shops have gone, the clothes in the remaining elegant boutiques are showpieces. Safer not to ask to try anything on. Probably not for sale.

In these years, the village has only marginally changed. Where villagers have left -or died, their sons and daughters now walk the same walks, and talk the same talk. The' sun will be out later' is a safe comment, and ' No wind today.'

The proprietor of the village shop, calling itself' Le Petit Marché, is still rushing in and out -moving hefty boxes of fruit and veg. four times a day. She looks a little older.

Other shops are, as always, opening now and again- and the pharmacy has rearranged its complete interior as usual. This time stock is mainly interesting tisanes, diffuser oils and sleeping potions.

Let's hope somebody sells sunblock.

The new plaques remind people of the past, pictures of flooded streets with boats being rowed down the middle, and groups of people carrying washing to public wash areas. There is a hand delivered, hand written paper with stories of past times.

The children who were children then, are now grown-up. One in particular stands out. He, a neighbours' grandson who helped the couple when they first arrived.

He taught the woman how to say ' pain' -it's pronounced more like 'pang' here. 'Vin and vent' were confusing too, both sounding the same.

Now, possibly with their influence, he lives in South East England and -only occasionally -returns.

Writing to the couple, he prefers England, 'people are more sociable, they don't judge you by the way you dress, the shops are open at all hours, you don't need lots of diplomas, buses come along every 15 minutes and- the police are friendly!' So far, his stay has been 13 years. He is happy.

The couple don't know if they will copy him and return....

Nobody likes endings, so the ending to this story hasn't been written yet, after all they need to wait for the flamingos to fly back.

Life. Henry Van Dyke

Let me but live from year to year,
With forward face and unreluctant soul;
Not hurrying to, nor turning from the goal;
Not mourning for the things that disappear
in the dim past, nor holding back in fear
from what the future veils, but with a whole
And happy heart that pays its toll
To Youth and Age, and travels on with cheer

So let the way wind up the hill or down,
O'er rough or smooth, the journey will be
joy,
Still seeking what I sought when but a boy.
New friendship, high adventure, and a crown,
My heart will keep the courage of the quest,
And hope the road's last turn will be the best.

Les Flamants roses.

Life and 'The Coming of Good Luck.' Robert Herrick

So good luck came, and on my roof did light,

Like noise-less snow, or as the dew of night:

Not all at once, but gently, as the trees

Are by the sun- beams, tickled by degrees.

Here is the other sky

Text Copyright © 2024 Wendy Lee. All rights reserved.

Illustrations Eleanora D'Amico

ISBN: 979-8326141439

Permission Acknowledgement 'Sea Fever' John Masefield 'Society of Authors as the Literary Representative of the Estate of John Masefield.

'Arrival' R. S. A. Thomas © Elodie Thomas

All reasonable efforts have been made to obtain copyright permission for information quoted and poetry reproduced in this book. If I have committed an oversight, I will be pleased to rectify it in a subsequent edition.

Poetry in the Public Domain 2024;

Max Ehrmann, W Davies, Emily Dickinson, William Carlos

Williams, Bashō. W. B. Yeats, Anna Akhmatova, Edna St. Vincent Millay. Henry Van Dyke. Robert Frost, Robert Herrick.

'French Days, French Voices' is a work of non-fiction. It chronicles twenty five years of daily living in a French village.

I am grateful to my French neighbours, friends and acquaintances, who wittingly, or sometimes unwittingly, provided the French voices of my story.

Special thanks for insights, corrections and, especially, kindness: Michèle Martin, Hélène and Eliane Léger, Claude Gerini, Roger Tissier, Cédric Armengaud, Aimé Tiné, La famille Granjeon, Taliercio and Minana.

I have been influenced by, and learned from ,the writings of

Annie Ernaux, 'Exteriors'

Lydia Davis, 'Can't and Won't.'

Theodore Zeldin 'The French'

Deborah Levy 'August Blue'.

Manufactured by Amazon.ca
Bolton, ON